SAY WHAT?

670 QUOTES THAT SHOULD
NEVER HAVE BEEN SAID

Library of Congress Cataloging-in-Publication Data available upon request.

ISBN: 978-1-946064-04-2

Illustration and design by Phillip Wells

duopress books are available at special discounts when purchased in bulk for sales promotions as well as for fund-raising or educational use. Special editions can be created to specification. Contact us at hello@duopressbooks.com for more information.

Manufactured in China
10 9 8 7 6 5 4 3 2 1

Duopress LLC
8 Market Place, Suite 300
Baltimore, MD 21202

Distributed by Workman Publishing Company, Inc.
Published simultaneously in Canada by Thomas Allen & Son Limited.

To order: hello@duopressbooks.com
www.punchlineideas.com
www.workman.com

SAY WHAT?

670 QUOTES THAT SHOULD
NEVER HAVE BEEN SAID

Doreen Chila-Jones

"Say What"

A term used when a person wishes for a surprising or astonishing statement to be repeated, or simply to show their surprise at said statement.

—Urban Dictionary.com

CONTENTS

Impertinent
POLITICAL PUNDITS

"Polls are for strippers and cross-country skiers."

—Sarah Palin

"It isn't pollution that's harming the environment. It's the impurities in our air and water that are doing it."
—Former U.S. vice president Al Gore

"I love California. I practically grew up in Phoenix."

"It is wonderful to be here in the great state of Chicago."

"I have made good judgments in the past. I have made good judgments in the future."

—Former U.S. vice president Dan Quayle

"I think that gay marriage is something that should be between a man and a woman." —Arnold Schwarzenegger

"I am not a crook." —President Richard Nixon

"It certainly doesn't look familiar to me, but I don't want to say with certitude to you something that I don't know to be the certain truth."

"This is not a national security matter. We're not making a federal case out of this... I'm not sure it rises—no pun intended—to that level."

"I was perhaps, forgive me, a little stiff yesterday."
>   —Former congressman
>   Anthony Weiner

"I've looked on a lot of women with lust. I've committed adultery in my heart many times."
—President Jimmy Carter, *Playboy* magazine

"Life is indeed precious, and I believe the death penalty helps affirm this fact."
—Former New York City mayor Edward Koch

"I haven't committed a crime. What I did was fail to comply with the law." —Former New York City mayor David Dinkins

....

"Outside of the killings, D.C. has one of the lowest crime rates in the country." —Former Washington, D.C., mayor Marion Barry

....

"Reports that say something hasn't happened are always interesting to me, because as **we know**, there **are known knowns**; there are things **we know we know**. We also **know** there are **known unknowns**; that is to say **we know** there are some things we **do not know**. But there are also **unknown unknowns**—the ones **we don't know we don't know**." —Former U.S. defense secretary Donald Rumsfeld

"You know the one thing that's wrong with this country? Everyone gets a chance to have their fair say."

"I never had sexual relations with that woman."

"That depends on what the meaning of 'is' is."

"A few years ago, this guy would have been getting us coffee." (speaking about Barack Obama)

"African Americans watch the same news at night that ordinary Americans do."

"When I was in England, I experimented with marijuana a time or two, and I didn't like it. I didn't inhale and never tried it again."

—President Bill Clinton

"If I didn't kick his ass every day, he wouldn't be worth anything." —Hillary Clinton, on Bill Clinton

"When the president does it, that means that it is not illegal."

"You know, I always wondered about that taping equipment but I'm damn glad we have it, aren't you?"

—President Richard Nixon

"The world is more like it is now than it ever has been before." —President Dwight Eisenhower

"A billion here, a billion there, sooner or later it adds up to real money." —Former congressman Everett Dirksen

"A guy comes in and puts a gun in my ribs. And I just said, 'I believe that you want the guy behind the counter.'" —Presidential candidate Ben Carson

"I've now been in 48 states—I think one left to go." —President Barack Obama

"Believe me, as a busy single mother…er, I shouldn't say single. When you have a husband who's president it can feel a little single…but he's there." —First Lady Michelle Obama

"The very first essential for success is a perpetually constant and regular employment of violence."

"What luck for rulers that men do not think."

"If you tell a big enough lie and tell it frequently enough, it will be believed."

"It is not the truth that matters, but victory."

—Adolf Hitler

"We don't necessarily discriminate. We simply exclude certain types of people." —Colonel Gerald Wellman, ROTC instructor

"Those who survived the San Francisco earthquake said, 'Thank God, I'm still alive.' But, of course, those who died, their lives will never be the same again."
—Former California senator Barbara Boxer

....

"You know what I heard...that it's not black on black crime that's killing kids in Chicago, it's actually cops shooting those kids."
—Monique Davis, Chicago Democrat

....

"Men often do need maternity care." —President Obama's Health and Human Services chief Kathleen Sebelius

"We have every mixture you can have. I have a black, a woman, two Jews and a cripple. And we have talent."
—James Watt, secretary of the Interior,
Reagan administration

"They're coming after your doughnuts!"
—Kentucky senator Rand Paul

"I have to confess that it's crossed my mind that you could not be a Republican and a Christian." —Hillary Clinton

"It had to do with Cuba and missiles, I'm pretty sure." —White House press secretary Dana Perino, admitting she had never heard of the Cuban Missile Crisis

"There is a mandate to impose a voluntary return to traditional values."

"Facts are stupid things."

"Well, I learned a lot...I went down to [Latin America] to find out from them and [learn] their views. You'd be surprised. They're all individual countries."

—President Ronald Reagan

"If Abraham Lincoln was alive today he would roll over in his grave." —President Gerald Ford

"Number one, I have great respect for women. I was the one that really broke the glass ceiling on behalf of women, more than anybody in the construction industry."

"You know it really doesn't matter what they write as long as you've got a young and beautiful piece of ass."

"Grab 'em by the pussy."

"Look at that face. Would anyone vote for that? Can you imagine that, the face of our next president? I mean, she's a woman, and I'm not s'posedta say bad things, but really, folks, come on. Are we serious?" (speaking about presidential candidate Carly Fiorina)

"I would bomb the sh*t out of them."

—Presidential candidate
Donald Trump

"You may have seen I recently launched a Snap-chat account. I love it. I love it. Those messages **disappear** all by themselves." —Hillary Clinton

"We should replace bilingual education with immersion in English so people learn the common language of the country and they learn the language of prosperity, not the language of living in a ghetto."

"Give the park police more ammo." (explaining what to do about the homeless problem a few days after the police shot and killed a homeless person in front of the White House)

"She isn't young enough or pretty enough to be the President's wife." (speaking of his ex-wife)

—Newt Gingrich, Former Speaker of the House

"I think Assad's invasion of Syria will be seen as a blunder." —Presidential candidate Martin O'Malley (Bashar al-Assad is, in fact, the president of Syria.)

"Our enemies are innovative and resourceful, and so are we. They never stop thinking about new ways to harm our country and our people, and neither do we."

"Goodbye from the world's biggest polluter." (speaking at his last G-8 Summit)

"Are you going to ask that question with shades on?" (talking to a blind reporter)

—President George W. Bush

"When we create diversity programs that include everyone, quote, 'of color,' other than whites, struggling whites like the families in the Appalachian mountains, we're not being true to the Democratic Party principles." —Former U.S. senator James Webb

"We'd like to avoid problems, because when we have problems, we can have troubles." —Wesley Bolin, former governor of Arizona

"Now, they're saying I groped a male staffer. Yes, I did. Not only did I grope him, I tickled him until he couldn't breathe and four guys jumped on top of me. It was my 50th birthday." —Eric Massa, former congressman

"Guess what this liberal would be all about? This liberal will be about socializing...uh, um...Would be about, basically, taking over, and the government running all of your companies." —Maxine Waters, congresswoman, on socialism

"You're not a member of the Taliban, are you?" —Chuck Hagel, former secretary of defense, taking a question from Robin Gandhi, a man of Indian descent

"The almighty certainly never intended that people should travel at such breakneck speed." —President Martin Van Buren, referring to new trains that could travel at 15 mph

"A nation of spaghetti eaters cannot restore Roman civilization!"

"Let us have a dagger between our teeth, a bomb in our hand, and an infinite scorn in our hearts."

"Three cheers for war, noble and beautiful above all."

—Benito Mussolini

"I have opinions of my own, strong opinions, but I don't always agree with them." —President George H.W. Bush

"So?" —Former vice president Dick Cheney, when asked his opinion of a recent poll showing that most Americans didn't believe the Iraq War was worth fighting

"The honorable Member is living proof that a pig's bladder on a stick can be elected to Parliament." —Tony Banks, Labour Party member of Parliament on Tory MP Terry Dicks

....

"I do think there are certain times we should infringe on your freedom."

—Former New York City mayor Michael Bloomberg

....

"White folks was in the caves while we [blacks] was building empires...We built pyramids before Donald Trump ever knew what architecture was...we taught philosophy and astrology and mathematics before Socrates and them Greek homos ever got around to it." —Civil rights activist Al Sharpton

"Any negative polls are fake news, just like the CNN, ABC, NBC polls in the election. Sorry, people want border security and extreme vetting."

"Happy New Year to all, including to my many enemies and those who have fought me and lost so badly they just don't know what to do. Love!"

"Meryl Streep, one of the most over-rated actresses in Hollywood, doesn't know me but attacked last night at the Golden Globes. She is a Hillary flunky who lost big. For the 100th time, I never 'mocked' a disabled reporter (would never do that) but simply showed him 'groveling' when he totally changed a 16 year old story that he had written in order to make me look bad. Just more very dishonest media!"

—President Donald Trump

"Our great African-American President hasn't exactly had a positive impact on the thugs who are so happily and openly destroying Baltimore."

"It's freezing and snowing in New York—we need global warming!"

"My IQ is one of the highest—and you all know it! Please don't feel so stupid or insecure; it's not your fault."

"My Twitter has become so powerful that I can actually make my enemies tell the truth."

—Presidential candidate
Donald Trump

"It's doubtful Russia will be invading Alaska anytime soon considering Russia cared so little about Alaska they sold it for 2 cents an acre. Come to think of it, with our current economic crisis, maybe we should just sell it back. It could be America's equivalent of selling all the DVDs you never watch on eBay to make some extra bucks after you've lost your job." —Vice presidential candidate Sarah Palin

"Sometimes people mistake the way I talk for what I am thinking."

"It's not for me. I tried human flesh and it's too salty for my taste."

—Idi Amin Dada,
former Ugandan president

"If you early voted, go vote again tomorrow. One more time's not going to hurt. Tomorrow we're going to elect [Democrat] Earl Tayor as [district attorney], so he won't prosecute you if you vote twice." —Don Cravins, mayor of Opelousas, Louisiana

"Death solves all problems—no man, no problem."

"It is enough that the people know there was an election. The people who cast the votes decide nothing. The people who count the votes decide everything."

"I want a new invincible human being, insensitive to pain, resistant, and indifferent to the quality of food they eat."

—Joseph Stalin

"A zebra does not change its spots."

"During my service in the United States Congress, I took the initiative in creating the Internet."

—Former vice president Al Gore

"These are ammunition, they're bullets, so the people who have those now, they're going to shoot them, so if you ban them in the future, the number of these high-capacity magazines is going to decrease dramatically over time because the bullets will have been shot and there won't be any more available."
—Diana DeGette, representative from Colorado, speaking about pistol or rifle ammo magazines, which can actually be used over and over again

"I mean you've got the first sort of mainstream African-American who is articulate and bright and clean and nice-looking guy." (speaking about Barack Obama)

"A man I'm proud to call my friend. A man who will be the next President of the United States—Barack America!"

"Stand up...Chuck, stand up, Chuck, let 'em see you!" (speaking to Missouri state senator Chuck Graham, who is wheelchair bound)

"You cannot go to a 7-11 or a Dunkin Donuts unless you have a slight Indian accent. I'm not joking!"

"Folks, I can tell you I've known eight presidents, three of them intimately."

—Joe Biden, vice president during the Obama administration

"I never took a position on Keystone until I took a position on Keystone."
—Hillary Clinton

. . . .

"In about 18 months from now, hopefully [Senator Vincent Sheheen] will have sent Nikki Haley back to wherever the hell she came from and this country can move forward."
—Dick Harpootlian, former South Carolina Democratic Party chairman, referring to Governor Nikki Haley's Indian heritage

. . . .

"You know, education, if you make the most of it, you study hard, you do your home-work and you make an effort to be smart, you can do well. If you don't, you get stuck in Iraq." —Former secretary of state John Kerry, speaking to the troops

"Jews should get the hell out of Palestine and go home [to Germany and Poland]."
—White House reporter Helen Thomas

"Spying has always gone on since ancient times."

"Nobody should have any illusion about the possibility of gaining military superiority over Russia. We will never allow this to happen."

"You must obey the law, always, not only when they grab you by your special place."

"I find it hard to believe that he rushed to some hotel to meet girls of loose morals, although ours are undoubtedly the best in the world." (talking about unsubstantiated accounts of some devious activities by Donald Trump during trips to Russia)

—Vladimir Putin

"We'll be deprived of women's beauty, because they'll be covered from head to toe… unfaithful women will be stoned and thieves will have their hands cut off. Women covering their face would mean an improvement for some, but there are few of them and I cannot see any such here." —Miloš Zeman, Czech president, speaking about female Muslim immigrants

---

"The Europe of today cannot be reformed in my opinion, there's nothing to be reformed in Brussels. It's run by a group of people who hate the Italian people and economy in particular." —Matteo Salvini, Italian member of the European Parliament

---

"Politics is when you say you are going to do one thing while intending to do another. Then you do neither what you said nor what you intended." —Saddam Hussein

"I wish Stanley Baldwin no ill, but it would have been much better if he had never lived." —Winston Churchill

"Tell him I can only deal with one sh*t at a time." —Winston Churchill, on being disturbed in his toilet by a call from the Lord Privy Seal

"Winston, if you were my husband I would flavour your coffee with poison." —Lady Astor, to Winston Churchill

"So many of the people in the arenas here were under-privileged anyway. This is working very well for them." —Barbara Bush, talking about people that found shelter in sports arenas during Hurricane Katrina

"Germany probably thinks its population is moribund, and it is probably seeking to lower wages and continue to recruit slaves through mass immigration."

"I'm not saying that the gas chambers didn't exist. I couldn't see them myself."

"Tolerance? What does that mean? I am a very tolerant and hospitable person, like you. Would you accept 12 illegal immigrants moving into your flat? You would not! On top of that, they start to remove the wallpaper! Some of them would steal your wallet and brutalize your wife. You would not accept that! Consequently, we are hospitable, but we decide with whom we want to be."

—Jean-Marie Le Pen, former leader of the French National Front party

"I don't care who does the electing, so long as I get to do the nominating." —William Magear Tweed, aka Boss Tweed, American politician

"If you had not committed great sins, God would not have sent a punishment like me upon you."

"The greatest happiness is to scatter your enemy and drive him before you. To see his cities reduced to ashes. To see those who love him shrouded and in tears. And to gather to your bosom his wives and daughters."

—Genghis Khan

"I don't want to be rude but, really, you have the charisma of a damp rag and the appearance of a low-grade bank clerk."—Nigel Farage, on European Council president Herman Van Rompuy

"The internet is a great way to get on the net. Life is very important to Americans." —Former senator Bob Dole

"I never knew how ugly and how stupid I was until, you know, we had Twitter."

"Most women say 'Please speak to me from the waist up: my brain, my eyes.'"

"Your job is not to call things ridiculous that are said by our press secretary and our president. That's not your job."

"You're saying it's a falsehood. And they're giving—Sean Spicer, our press secretary—gave alternative facts."

—Kellyanne Conway,
senior White House advisor
to President Donald Trump

"Alternative facts aren't facts, they are falsehoods." —Chuck Todd, NBC's *Meet the Press*

"This was the largest audience to ever witness an inauguration, period." —Sean Spicer, White House press secretary

"The legitimate powers of government extend to such acts only as are injurious to others. It does me no injury for my neighbor to say there are twenty gods or no god. It neither picks my pocket nor breaks my leg." —President Thomas Jefferson

"He doesn't dye his hair   he's just prematurely orange." —President Gerald Ford, on Ronald Reagan

"Religion is excellent stuff for keeping common people quiet. Religion is what keeps the poor from murdering the rich."
—Napoléon Bonaparte

"You've got a duty to die and get out of the way. Let the other society, our kids, build a reasonable life." —Former Colorado governor Dick Lamm, arguing that sick, elderly people have the right to physician-assisted suicide

"I am clearly more popular than Reagan. I am in my third term. Where's Reagan? Gone after two! Defeated by George Bush and Michael Dukakis no less." —Marion Barry, former mayor of Washington, D.C.

Animated
ANARCHY

"Don't do drugs, kids. There is a time and place for everything. It's called college."

—Chef, *South Park*

"Obviously I'm dealing with inferior mentalities."

"Poor Bugs. But any way you look at it, it's better he should suffer. After all, it was me or him, and, obviously, it couldn't be me. It's a simple matter of logic. I'm not like other people. I can't stand pain. It hurts me."

"Consequences, shmonsequences, as long as I'm rich."

"I demand that you shoot me now!"

—Daffy Duck

"I shall now attempt to eat a diet lunch consisting of one leaf of lettuce lightly seasoned with...one quart of mayonnaise." —Garfield

"Oh, I'm sorry. I guess I skipped the Emily Post chapter on how to introduce your mother to a hooker." —Sterling Archer, *Archer*

"Let me let you in on a little secret, Charlie Brown. If you really want to impress people, you need to show them you're a winner. Of course, when I say 'you,' you know I don't mean 'you personally.'" —Lucy Van Pelt, *Peanuts* by Charles Schultz

"My God, you've gotten fat."
—Edna Mode, *The Incredibles*

"Dear Santa, you are a bitch nigga. No, scratch that. Dear Santa, you are a bitch *ass* nigga. I heard they hired extra security to protect you. That's a bitch move, Santa. I'm coming for that ass again. Until you pay what you owe. Sincerely yours, The Santa Stalker." —Riley, *The Boondocks*

"I want to build two little caskets and give her tits a tasteful, dignified funeral."
—*The Venture Brothers*

"What the hell kind of country is this where I can only hate a man if he's white?"

"You know, Helen Keller was largely useless, but look how we remember her. Yep, First Lady of the American stage."

"The only woman I'm pimping is sweet lady propane! And I'm tricking her out all over this town."

"Why would anyone smoke weed when they could just mow a lawn?"

"Maybe I should tie the long hair on your head to the short hair on your ass and kick you down the street!"

—Hank Hill, *King of the Hill*

"Lisa, if you don't like your job you don't strike. You just go in every day and do it really half-assed. That's the American way."

"What do we need a psychiatrist for? We know our kid is nuts."

"Remember that postcard Grandpa sent us from Florida of that alligator biting that woman's bottom? That's right, we all thought it was hilarious. But, it turns out we were wrong. That alligator was sexually harassing that woman."

—Homer Simpson, *The Simpsons*

"Perform for the troops? Why should I? What have they ever done for me?"
—Krusty the Clown, *The Simpsons*

"Oh I feel so delightfully white trash. Mommy, I want a mullet." —Stewie Griffin, *Family Guy*

"By the way, Lois, I got a piercing over there. I'm not going to tell you where but I will give you a hint— it wasn't on my nose or my ear and it was one of my balls." —Peter Griffin, *Family Guy*

"I just don't trust anything that bleeds for five days and doesn't die." —Mr. Garrison, *South Park*, talking about women and menstruation

"All right, all right, make like Siamese twins and split...And then one of you die."
—Peter Griffin, *Family Guy*

"You're speechless, I see. A fine quality in a wife." —Jafar, *Aladdin*

"I warn you, child. If I lose my temper, you lose your head! Understand?!"
—Queen of Hearts, *Alice in Wonderland*

"You so much as TOUCH kitty's ass, and I'll put a firecracker in your nutsack and blow your balls all over your pants."

"It's a man's obligation to stick his boneration in a women's separation; this sort of penetration will increase the population of the younger generation."

"How 'bout we sing, 'Kyle's mom is a stupid bitch' in D Minor."

—Eric Cartman, *South Park*

"Dude, you just pumped in my face!" —Craig, *Sanjay and Craig*

"Ohh, are you upset or something? I said you had diabetes, not cry-a-betes." —Dr. Weisman, *King of the Hill*

"Now, if you'll excuse me, I, Mojo Jojo, have a town to take over. I have a world to conquer. I have to seize control of an area and force its inhabitants to follow my way of thinking." —Mojo Jojo, *The Powerpuff Girls*

"And all of the young 'uns are waiting with glee, thinking only of morn and what's under that tree. And not just the children, the teenagers, too. Chuck wants a football, Kathleen a tattoo." —Narrator, *The Powerpuff Girls*

"Did you hear that, Meg? Guys can marry other guys now. So... this is awkward, but I mean, if they can do that, that is pretty much it for you, isn't it? I mean you might as well pack it in. Game over." —Stewie, *Family Guy*

"I haven't seen an Englishman take a blow like that since Hugh Grant!"

"I haven't seen a Jew run like that since Poland, 1938!"

—Sportscaster Frank, *South Park*

"I was 14, just a little older than Bobby. But I knew Uncle Sam needed me, so I lied and signed up. We had beat the Nazzys in Italy, and they shipped me to the Pacific theater. A Tojo torpedo sent our troop ship to the bottom. I could only save three of my buddies: Fatty, Stinky, and Brooklyn. They were kind of like you fellas, only one of them was from Brooklyn. Out of the sun came a Tojo Zero and put fitty bullets in my back. The blood attracted sharks. I had to give 'em Fatty. Then things took a turn for the worse. I made it to an island, but it was full of Tojos! They were spitting on the U.S. flag! So I rushed 'em, but it was a trap. They opened fire and blew my shins off. Last thing I remember, I beat 'em all to death with a big piece of Fatty. I woke up in a field hospital, and they were sewing my feet to my knees." —Cotton, *King of the Hill*

"Kamp Krusty is built on an ancient Indian burial ground. We've got archery, wallet-making, the whole megillah! And for all you fat kids, my exclusive program of diet and ridicule will really get results!"
—Krusty the Clown, *The Simpsons*

"**Genetic engineering is man's way of correcting God's hideous mistakes, like German people.**"

"Gay people, well, gay people are EVIL. Evil right down to their cold black hearts which pump not blood like yours or mine, but rather, a thick, vomitous oil that oozes through their rotten veins and clots in their pea-sized brains; which becomes the cause of their Nazi-esque patterns of violent behavior. Do you understand?"

—Mr. Garrison, *South Park*

"Hello and welcome to Bob's Burgers. The burger of the day is 'The Child Molester,' it comes with candy."

"You're the worst kind of autistic."

—Louise Belcher, *Bob's Burgers*

"I taught my fart to be patriotic. It's Stinky Doodle Dandy!" —Gene, *Bob's Burgers*

"You little pantywads think you're ready to play the Wolves again? The Wolves eat razorblades for breakfast! Run, you bunch of pudgy-butted softies! Run, with your fancy sneakers with pumps, valves and lights on the back that can set off a seizure! But what do you care? I ran around the world in a pair of Chuck Taylors for the love of pete! Take a salt tablet." —Coach Sauers, *King of the Hill*

"Check out that guy. Why is his face all twisted up like that? Looks like he jacks off with Icy Hot. He looks like he just sh*t a gerbil!" —Ed Wuncler, *The Boondocks*

"Lord, please pray for the soul of this bitch. And guide my pimp hand and make it strong, Lord. So that she might learn a ho's place. Amen." —A pimp named Slickback, *The Boondocks*

"My own pony! I'm gonna name him Sammy Davis Jr. the Pony." —Jazmine Dubois, *The Boondocks*

"Any noise, and I will butt-rape your grandfather with this broomstick! —Luna, *The Boondocks*

"Nowadays people think ho, ho, ho is the Hilton sisters standing next to Nicole Richie!" —Jazmine Dubois, *The Boondocks*

"It's like the N-word and the C-word had a baby and it was raised by all the bad words for Jews."

"Alright, Morty, don't break an arm jerking yourself off."

—Rick, *Rick and Morty*

"Lana, your eyes are amazing, I mean not compared to your tits, but..." —Sterling Archer, *Archer*

"You killed a black astronaut, Cyril! That's like killing a unicorn!" —Sterling Archer, *Archer*

"I'm no hero, I put my bra on one boob at a time like everyone else." —Tina Belcher, *Bob's Burgers*

Salty
CELEBRITIES

" Cartooning requires
a sense of humor and too
often a woman lacks that. "

—Walt Disney

"People think I have changed, and I have changed. I'm now the person I know I am."
—Jon Gosselin, *Jon & Kate Plus 8*

"The only happy artist is a dead artist, because only then you can't change. After I die, I'll probably come back as a paintbrush." —Sylvester Stallone

"I'm not anorexic. I'm from Texas. Are there people from Texas that are anorexic? I've never heard of one. And that includes me."
—Jessica Simpson

"I make Jessica Simpson look like a rock scientist." —Tara Reid

"I've never really wanted to go to Japan. Simply because I don't like eating fish. And I know that's very popular out there in Africa." —Britney Spears

"Whenever I watch TV and see those poor starving kids all over the world, I can't help but cry I mean I'd love to be skinny like that, but not with all those flies and death and stuff."
—Mariah Carey

"It's not that I dislike many people. It's just that I don't like many people."
 —Bryant Gumbel

"I look at modeling as something I'm doing for black people in general."
—Naomi Campbell

"When I'm really hot, I can walk into a room and if a man doesn't look at me, he's probably gay."
—Kathleen Turner

"He speaks English, Spanish, and he's bilingual, too." —Don King

"Everything bad that can happen to a person has happened to me."

"There's nobody in the world like me. I think every decade has an iconic blonde, like Marilyn Monroe or Princess Diana and, right now, I'm that icon."

—Paris Hilton

"I've never been drunk in my life. I don't use recreational drugs." —Paula Abdul

"I spoke to a girl today who had cancer and we were talking about how this is such a hard thing for her, but it taught her a big lesson on who her friends are and so much about life. She's 18. And I was like, that's how I feel." —Kim Kardashian

"I just let my hair go—if there's no hairdresser around I really can't be bothered!"
—Khloe Kardashian

"The Supreme Court has ruled that they cannot have a nativity scene in Washington, D.C. This wasn't for any religious reasons. They couldn't find three wise men and a virgin." —Jay Leno

"Who knew that the devil had a factory where he made millions of fossils, which his minions distributed throughout the earth, in order to confuse my tiny brain?" —Comedian Lewis Black

"All of a sudden, you're like the Bin Laden of America. Osama bin Laden is the only one who knows what I'm going through." —R. Kelly, R&B crooner.

"I can't believe my grand mothers making me take Out the garbage I'm rich f*** this I'm going home I don't need this sh*t." —Rapper 50 Cent, on Twitter

"How can mirrors be real if our eyes aren't real"

"School is the tool to brainwash the youth"

"If newborn babies could speak they would be the most intelligent beings on planet earth"

"Trees are never sad look at them every once in awhile there quite beautiful"

"If everybody in the world dropped out of school we would have a much more intelligent society"

—Jaden Smith, on Twitter

"First my mother was Spanish. Then she became a Jehovah's Witness." —Geri Halliwell, "Ginger Spice" of the Spice Girls

"It's put everything into perspective. I have a different respect now for people who don't have legs." —Jessie J, British pop singer, after breaking her foot

"Now I can say that I still haven't had an abortion, but I wish I had." —Lena Dunham

"What are you looking at, sugar tits?" —Mel Gibson, to a female police officer after being arrested in 2006.

"I'm tired of people not treating me like the gift that I am." —Paula Abdul

"I have this weird thing that if I sleep with someone they're going to take my creativity from me through my vagina."

"I don't know if this is too much…but I can actually mentally give myself an orgasm."

—Lady Gaga

"Elizabeth Taylor's so fat, she puts mayonnaise on her aspirins." —Joan Rivers

....

"The only time my wife and I had a simultaneous orgasm was when the judge signed the divorce papers." —Woody Allen

....

"Michael Jackson's album was called Bad because there wasn't enough room on the sleeve for Pathetic." —Prince

"@justinbieber what do you feed that thing. #proud daddy." —Justin Bieber's dad, about Justin's penis, on Twitter

"I actually don't like thinking. I think people think I like to think a lot. And I don't. I don't like to think." —Kanye West

"Fiction writing is great. You can make up almost anything." —Ivanka Trump

"I do believe that I deserve what I have. I don't think I'm entitled to it. That's a big difference."
—Adam Levine

"I don't think there is anything particularly wrong about hitting a woman—although I don't recommend doing it in the same way that you'd hit a man. An openhanded slap is justified—if all other alternatives fail and there has been plenty of warning. If a woman is a bitch, or hysterical, or bloody-minded continually, then I'd do it. I think a man has to be slightly advanced, ahead of the woman." —Sean Connery

"But you know how Prince had a lot of girls back in the day? Prince was, like, the guy. I'm just that, today. But most women won't have any complaints if they've been with me. They can't really complain. It's all good." —Chris Brown

"It's really hard to maintain a one-on-one relationship if the other person is not going to allow me to be with other people." —Axl Rose

"As soon as I hear there is a famous penis out there, I am the first person to ravenously devour it online." —Seth Rogen

"I love my tits being out. It's like, one of my things, I guess." —Kendall Jenner, model

"Bill Clinton is a man who thinks international affairs means dating a girl from out of town."
—Tom Clancy, author

"I never worry about diets. The only carrots that interest me are the number you get in a diamond."

"Marriage is a great institution, but I'm not ready for an institution."

"It ain't no sin if you crack a few laws now and then, just so long as you don't break any."

—Mae West

"So Carol, you're a housewife and mother. And have you got any children?" —Michael Barrymore

"If it weren't for electricity we'd all be watching television by candlelight." —George Gobel

"If Jesus came back and saw what was being done in his name, he'd never stop throwing up."

"Photons have mass? I didn't even know they were Catholic."

—Woody Allen

"Don't talk to me." —Rachael Ray

"I would rather die than let my kid eat Cup-a-Soup." —Gwyneth Paltrow

"I've always thought Marilyn Monroe looked fabulous, but I'd kill myself if I was that fat." —Elizabeth Hurley

"What is this c*nt doing on the cover of Rolling Stone? Music has officially died."
—Sinéad O'Connor on Kim Kardashian's *Rolling Stone* cover

"No one ever expects a great lay to pay all of the bills."

"I like to wake up each morning feeling a new man."

"Underwear makes me uncomfortable. And besides, my parts have to breathe."

"When you lie down with dogs, you get up with fleas."

"Must I always wear a low-cut dress to be important?"

—Jean Harlow,
1930s Hollywood bombshell

"Hollywood always wanted me to be pretty, but I fought for realism."

"Everybody has a heart...except some people."

"From the moment I was six I felt sexy. And let me tell you it was hell, sheer hell, waiting to do something about it."

"I never did pal around with the actresses. Their talk usually bored me to tears."

"I'd marry again if I found a man who had fifteen million dollars, would sign over half to me, and guarantee that he'd be dead within a year."

"In this business, until you're known as a monster, you're not a star."

"I wouldn't piss on Joan Crawford if she were on fire."

—Bette Davis

"Poor Bette! She looks like she's never had a happy day…or night!…in her life."

"I don't hate Bette Davis, even though the press wants me to; I resent her. I don't see how she built a career out of mannerisms instead of real acting ability. She's a phony, but I guess the public likes that."

—Joan Crawford, on Bette Davis

"She has slept with every male star at MGM except Lassie."

"Why am I so good at playing bitches? I think it's because I'm not a bitch. Maybe that's why Miss Crawford always plays ladies."

—Bette Davis, on Joan Crawford

"She ran the whole gamut of the emotions from A to B." —Dorothy Parker, on Audrey Hepburn's acting in a play

"Well, at least he has found his true love—what a pity he can't marry himself." —Frank Sinatra, on Robert Redford

"She speaks five languages and can't act in any of them." —British actor Sir John Gielgud, on *Casablanca* star Ingrid Bergman

"The easiest way for you to lose 10 pounds is just to take off your wig." —Madonna, to Elton John

"If you kick every Latino out of this country, then who is going to be cleaning your toilets, Donald Trump?" —Kelly Osbourne

"I am on a drug. It's called Charlie Sheen. It's not available because if you try it once, you will die. Your face will melt off and your children will weep over your exploded body." —Charlie Sheen

"You don't know anything about the history of journalism, psychology, or my life... You can't handle the truth."

"These drugs are dangerous. I have actually helped people come off. When you talk about postpartum, you can take people today, women, and what you do is you use vitamins. There is a hormonal thing that is going on, scientifically, you can prove that. But when you talk about emotional, chemical imbalances in people, there is no science behind that. You can use vitamins to help a woman through those things."

—Tom Cruise

"Active shooting in Canada, or as we call it in America, Wednesday."
—American model Chrissy Teigen, tweeting about a gun shooting in Ontario

"Please welcome—the wickedly talented, one and only—Adele Dazeem." —John Travolta, introducing actress Idina Menzel at the Oscars

"Not trying to be arrogant, but if I walked down the street and a girl saw me, she might take a look back because maybe I'm good-looking, right?"

"So remember, this is Bieber's world. You're just living in it. Bieber or die."

"A girl could be sitting on her computer, trying to get noticed by me, and not knowing she's the future Mrs. Justin Bieber."

—Justin Bieber

"I hate Americans. I hate America." —Ariana Grande, caught on a security camera in a donut shop

"Chris Brown beat you because you're not pretty enough." —Amanda Bynes, to Rihanna on Twitter

"It's not like nobody here hasn't already seen my boobs." —Dakota Johnson, joking about presenter Leslie Mann nearly causing her to have a wardrobe malfunction onstage

"It's work having a vagina. Guys don't think that it's work, but it is. You think it shows up like that to the event? It doesn't. Every night, it's like getting it ready for its first quinceañera. Believe me."

"I usually feel pretty good about myself. I know what I look like. You'd bang me, but you wouldn't blog about it... it's fine."

"Tonight I have one goal, and that was to just be able to take my underwear off at the end of the night and have it not look like I blew my nose in it."

—Amy Schumer

"I am not a demon. I am a lizard, a shark, a heat-seeking panther. I want to be Bob Denver on acid playing the accordion." —Nicholas Cage

"I don't care if Scarlett Johansson is buck naked on the 89th floor in a plate of ribs, I'm not going in there." —Chris Rock, on refusing to go into New York's Freedom Tower

....

"Alcohol may be man's worst enemy, but the bible says love your enemy." —Frank Sinatra

....

"The reason people use a crucifix against vampires is because vampires are allergic to bullsh*t."
—Richard Pryor

"Yes, I'm angry, yes, I'm outraged, yes, I have thought an awful lot about blowing up the White House, but I know that this won't change anything." —Madonna, at the Women's March on Washington

"Yes, reason has been a part of organized religion, ever since two nudists took dietary advice from a talking snake."

"Religion. It's given people hope in a world torn apart by religion."

—Jon Stewart

"For me to say I wasn't a genius, I would just be lying to you and to myself." —Kanye West

"Here's all you need to know about men and women: Women are crazy and men are stupid. And the reason women are crazy is that men are stupid." —George Carlin

"Religion has actually convinced people that there's an invisible man living in the sky who watches everything you do, every minute of every day. And the invisible man has a special list of ten things he does not want you to do. And if you do any of these ten things, he has a special place, full of fire and smoke and burning and torture and anguish, where he will send you to live and suffer and burn and choke and scream and cry forever and ever 'til the end of time! But He loves you. He loves you, and He needs money! He always needs money! He's all-powerful, all-perfect, all-knowing, and all-wise, somehow just can't handle money!"

—George Carlin

"I'm not sure about the parties. But whatever they have in Korea, that's bad." —Justin Bieber, on politics

"I think that the film Clueless was very deep. I think it was deep in the way that it was very light. I think lightness has to come from a very deep place if it's true lightness." —Alicia Silverstone

"There's a big difference between kneeling down and bending over."

"The essence of Christianity is told to us in the Garden of Eden history. The fruit that was forbidden was on the tree of knowledge. The subtext is, All the suffering you have is because you wanted to find out what was going on. You could be in the Garden of Eden if you had just kept your f***ing mouth shut and hadn't asked any questions."

—Frank Zappa

"Here's an easy way to figure out if you're in a cult: If you're wondering whether you're in a cult, the answer is yes." —Stephen Colbert, *I Am America*

"One of my biggest Achilles' heels has been my ego. And if I, Kanye West, can remove my ego, I think there's hope for everyone."

"I am God's vessel. But my greatest pain in life is that I will never be able to see myself perform live."

"Sometimes people write novels and they just be so wordy and so self-absorbed. I am not a fan of books. I would never want a book's autograph. I am a proud non-reader of books."

"I don't even listen to rap. My apartment is too nice to listen to rap in."

—Kanye West

Pious
IMPERTINENCE

"I think the world is being much helped by the suffering of the poor people."

—Mother Teresa

"Many of those people involved in Adolf Hitler were Satanists. Many were homosexuals. The two things seem to go together."

"The feminist agenda is not about equal rights for women. It is about a socialist, anti-family political movement that encourages women to leave their husbands, kill their children, practice witchcraft, destroy capitalism and become lesbians."

"I would warn Orlando that you're right in the way of some serious hurricanes, and I don't think I'd be waving those flags in God's face if I were you...It'll bring about terrorist bombs; it'll bring earthquakes, tornadoes, and possibly a meteor." (on Walt Disney World's "Gay Days")

—Pat Robertson, Southern Baptist leader

"Hearing nuns' confessions is like being stoned to death with popcorn." —Fulton J. Sheen, American archbishop

....

"Is God willing to prevent evil, but not able? Then he is not omnipotent. Is he able, but not willing? Then he is malevolent. Is he both able and willing? Then whence cometh evil? Is he neither able nor willing? Then why call him God?" —Greek philosopher Epicurus

....

"A celibate clergy is an especially good idea, because it tends to suppress any hereditary propensity toward fanaticism." —Carl Sagan

"Writing for a penny a word is ridiculous. If a man really wanted to make a million dollars, the best way would be to start his own religion." —L. Ron Hubbard, founder of Scientology

"I'm an atheist and I thank God for it." —George Bernard Shaw

"The word and works of God is quite clear, that women were made either to be wives or prostitutes."

"Men have broad and large chests, and small narrow hips, and more understanding than women, who have but small and narrow breasts, and broad hips, to the end they should remain at home, sit still, keep house, and bear and bring up children."

"What harm could it do if a man told a good lusty lie in a worthy cause and for the sake of the Christian Churches?"

—Martin Luther, reformer (1483–1546)

"Anyone who thinks sitting in church can make you a Christian must also think that sitting in a garage can make you a car." —Author Garrison Keillor

"The God of the Old Testament is arguably the most unpleasant character in all fiction: jealous and proud of it; a petty, unjust, unforgiving control-freak; a vindictive, bloodthirsty ethnic cleanser; a misogynistic, homophobic, racist, infanticidal, genocidal, filicidal, pestilential, megalomaniacal, sadomasochistic, capriciously malevolent bully." —Richard Dawkins, ethologist and author

"Is man merely a mistake of God's? Or God merely a mistake of man?" —Friedrich Nietzsche

"One would go mad if one took the Bible seriously; but to take it seriously one must be already mad." —Aleister Crowley, British occultist

"When one person suffers from a delusion, it is called insanity. When many people suffer from a delusion it is called a Religion." —Robert M. Pirsig, American writer and philosopher

"Religious liberty might be supposed to mean that everybody is free to discuss religion. In practice it means that hardly anybody is allowed to mention it." —G. K. Chesterton, British author

"With or without religion, good people can behave well and bad people can do evil; but for good people to do evil—that takes religion." —Steven Weinberg, Nobel laureate in physics

"The president of the United States has claimed, on more than one occasion, to be in dialogue with God. If he said that he was talking to God through his hairdryer, this would precipitate a national emergency. I fail to see how the addition of a hairdryer makes the claim more ridiculous or offensive." —Sam Harris, American author and philosopher

"The Bible tells us to be like God, and then on page after page it describes God as a mass murderer. This may be the single most important key to the political behavior of Western Civilization." —Robert Anton Wilson, American author

"Religion is for people who're afraid of going to hell. Spirituality is for those who've already been there." —Vine Deloria Jr., Native American author

"Better to sleep with a sober cannibal than a drunk Christian." —Herman Melville, American author

"If there is a God, atheism must seem to Him as less of an insult than religion." —Edmond de Goncourt, French author

"When we get through with the Jews in America, they'll think the treatment they received in Germany was nothing." —Father Charles E. Coughlin

"Every time I have wanted to tell the truth—that I have no faith—the words just do not come—my mouth remains closed. And yet I still keep on smiling at God and all." —Mother Teresa

"Thank God for the tsunami, and thank God that two thousand dead Swedes are fertilizing the ground over there [in Asia]. How many of these two thousand, do you suppose, were fags and dykes? This is how the Lord deals with His enemies. And the Lord has got some enemies. And Sweden heads the list. You filthy Swedes. You filthy Swedes!"

"Thank God for 9/11. Thank God that, five years ago, the wrath of God was poured out upon this evil nation. America, land of the sodomite damned. We thank thee, Lord God Almighty, for answering the prayers of those that are under the altar."

—Fred Phelps, American Baptist minister

"It is better for a girl to marry in such a time when she would begin menstruation at her husband's house rather than her father's home. Any father marrying his daughter so young will have a permanent place in heaven."

"If one commits the act of sodomy with a cow, an ewe, or a camel, their urine and their excrements become impure, and even their milk may no longer be consumed. The animal must then be killed and as quickly as possible and burned."

"Americans are the great Satan, the wounded snake."

—Ayatollah Khomeini

Trifling Duo
TV & MOVIES

"Did your mother put the whiskey in the baby bottle, or did she just mix it in with the dog food she fed you?"

—Nicky,
Orange Is the New Black

"Hey, so you know how I've always had a thing for half-Asians? Well, now I have a new favorite: Lebanese girls. Lebanese girls are the new half-Asians." —Barney Stinson, *How I Met Your Mother*

"Pretty women make us buy beer. Ugly women make us drink beer." —Al Bundy, *Married with Children*

"Okay, then let's talk about your daddy. Your daddy was so fat...that when he went to school he sat next to everybody! And still...he still not as fat as your fat mama!" —George Jefferson, *The Jeffersons*

"You are so ugly that if you pressed your face in some dough...you'd have gorilla cookies."
—Fred Sanford, *Sanford and Son*

"My body is very attracted to your body, but when you speak, my brain gets angry." —Mindy Lahiri, *The Mindy Project*

"Welcome to our home, as yous people say, 'Shaboom.'" (referring to the Jewish greeting "shalom")

"Why don't you go to sleep and dream about the tragedy that is your life."

—Archie Bunker, *All in the Family*

"My mom always said that if the Protestants catch a Catholic in their church, they feed them to the Jews." —Kate O'Brien, *The Drew Carey Show*

"Somewhere in the world, there's a very lucky girl...who's gonna date the lesbian you'll create tonight." —Mimi Bobeck, *The Drew Carey Show*

♪♪♪♪ "London Bridge is falling down, falling down, falling down. London Bridge is falling down, the Limeys built it wrong." ♪♪♪♪

"Now along comes this colored cop, see, and he wants to take over the mouth-to-mouth, but I'm thinking fast. I say no, I send him for the ambulance, you know, because if you give a person the wrong breath type, you could kill that person."

"God, we can't take no four dollars out of a pathetic check like that. That's your weekly pay? That's terrible. Geez, your boss must be an awful thief there. That's the same as I give my illegals out in the kitchen."

—Archie Bunker, *Archie Bunker's Place*

"Are you kidding me? Kukudio is a suspect and I'm not? Heck I killed a cop with his own gun. Oh. Wait...Did I get caught for that? [sighs] I'm getting old." —Frieda, *Orange Is the New Black*

"Listen, if your mind is starting to go, just tell me and I'll mercy break your neck, so you don't end up in Psych." —Gloria, *Orange Is the New Black*

"You know, if you're gonna poop in the shower, at least you could plan ahead. Like, do it in a shower cap, and take it with you after. Just common decency." —Lorna, *Orange Is the New Black*

"This food looks like something a walrus would regurgitate to feed its least favorite baby." —Alex, *Orange Is the New Black*

"Because I wear protection, so I haven't caught whatever form of syphilis you have that caused your soul to rot." —Caputo, *Orange Is the New Black*

....

"Maybe you should stop punishing yourself. I mean, what does a good mother do? A good mother does what's best for her children. And maybe what was best for your children was wipin' 'em out before they had to lead miserable f***ing lives."—Big Boo, *Orange Is the New Black*

....

"I've masturbated. There was this statue of Jesus that was especially ripped. That was my guy." —Sister Ingalls, *Orange Is the New Black*

"Snazzy told me a story about a girl named Piper. She could blow out candles with her coochie."—Inmate, *Orange Is the New Black*

"You can only vote within your race or your group. Look, just pretend it's the 1950s. It's easier to understand." —Nicky, *Orange Is the New Black*

"Lesbians can be very dangerous. It's the testosterone." —Healy, *Orange Is the New Black*

"All I wanted was to eat the chicken that is smarter than the other chickens and to absorb its power. And make a nice Kiev." —Galina "Red" Reznikov, *Orange Is the New Black*

"Lets have the type of night where it's like 5 a.m. and one of us has definitely punched someone who's been on a Disney Channel Show." —Elijah Krantz, *Girls*

"You're a sexist, egotistical, lying, hypocritical bigot." —Judy, *9 to 5*

"People have judged me because of my eyebrow. I can't control my eyebrow. I can't control it. I can't control what's on my face 24/7." —Tierra, *The Bachelor*

"Hey, Twitter Twat, WTF?" —Janine Skorsky, *House of Cards*

"You know who wears sunglasses inside? Blind people. And douche bags." —Dean Winchester, *Supernatural*

"You are the worst thing to happen to this country since food in buckets. And maybe slavery!" —Amy, *Veep*

"Then it's settled. Amy's birthday present will be my genitals." —Sheldon Cooper, *The Big Bang Theory*

"I know violence isn't the answer. But, yes it is." —Drita D'Avanzo, *Mob Wives*

"You are going to die tomorrow, Lord Bolton. Sleep well." —Sansa, *Game of Thrones*

"Now, since it's my last night on shore for a while, I'm going to go f*** the tits off this one." —Yara, *Game of Thrones*

"I'm here to help. Don't eat the help." —Tyrion, *Game of Thrones*

"Watching your vicious bastard die gave me more relief that a thousand lying whores." —Tyrion, *Game of Thrones*

....

"I shouldn't make jokes. My mother taught me not to throw stones at cripples. But my father taught me, aim for their head." —Ramsay Bolton, *Game of Thrones*

....

"Your king says he betrayed me for love. I say he betrayed me for firm tits and a tight fit... and I can respect that." —Walder Frey, *Game of Thrones*

"Any man dies with a clean sword, I'll rape his f***ing corpse!" —The Hound, *Game of Thrones*

"Has anyone ever told you you're as boring as you are ugly? —Jaime Lannister, *Game of Thrones*

"My frickin' vagina's sweating." —Madison Montgomery, *American Horror Story*

"Normally we've got naked coochies lined up along the sink, but it's slow." —Betty DiMello, *Masters of Sex*

"So stop looking at me with those watery turd eyes and get me a wedding dress, bitch." —Brittany, *Unreal*

"I am drawing a 50 mile radius around this house and if you so much as open your fly to urinate I will destroy you." —Trudy Campbell, *Mad Men*

"Don't you know a VIP when you see one? Your boss came out of my V and her Daddy's P so show a little respect for her Mama." —Ophelia, *How to Get Away with Murder*

"Here's a quick announcement that tryouts for this year's cheerleading squad are about to begin. We all know nothing makes a cheerleader more nervous than when she's late!" —Principal McGee, *Grease: Live*

"I'd be honored to be your maid of honor! And not just because my main competition is in a coma 'til I die." —Kat Graham, *The Vampire Diaries*

"Love is just a chemical reaction that compels animals to breed. It hits hard, Morty, then it slowly fades, leaving you stranded in a failing marriage. I did it, your parents are going to do it." —Rick, *Rick and Morty*

"A 22-year-old girl is like a good carpenter. No wood gets wasted." —Charlie Harper, *Two and a Half Men*

"I'm Jewish, my people invented circumcision. You're welcome." —Howard Wolowitz, *The Big Bang Theory*

"Don't get a man, get a dog. They're loyal and they die sooner." —Penny, *Charmed*

Movies

"You are a sad strange little man, and you have my pity." —Buzz Lightyear, *Toy Story*

"If I wanted a joke, I'd follow you into the john and watch you take a leak." —Neal Page, *Planes, Trains and Automobiles*

"You are nothing! If you were in my toilet I wouldn't bother flushing it. My bathmat means more to me than you." —Buddy Ackerman, *Swimming with Sharks*

"You pompous, stuck-up, snot-nosed, English, giant, twerp, scumbag, f***-face, d***head, a**hole." —Otto, *A Fish Called Wanda*

"I don't give a tuppenny f*** about your moral conundrum, you meat-headed sh*t sack." —Bill "The Butcher" Cunning, *Gangs of New York*

"You're an emotional f***ing cripple. Your soul is dog sh*t. Every single f***ing thing about you is ugly." —Marcus, *Bad Santa*

"It looks to me like the best part of you ran down the crack of your momma's ass and ended up as a brown stain on the mattress!" —Gunnery Sergeant Hartman, *Full Metal Jacket*

"You clinking, clanking, clattering collection of caliginous junk!" —The Wizard, *The Wizard of Oz*

"Even if I were blind, desperate, starved and begging for it on a desert island, you'd be the last thing I'd ever f***." —**Elvira Hancock,** *Scarface*

"You're somewhere between a cockroach and that white stuff that accumulates at the corner of your mouth when you're really thirsty. But, in your case, I'll make an exception." —Cyrus Grissom, *Con Air*

"Whose kitty litter did I just sh*t in?" —Wade Wilson, *Deadpool*

"When I watch you eat. When I see you asleep. When I look at you lately, I just want to smash your face in." —Barbara Rose, *The War of the Roses*

....

"What, you think you like me? You ain't like me motherf***er, you a punk. I've been with made people, connected people. Who've you been with? Chain-snatching, jive-ass, maricon motherf***ers. Why don't you get out of here and go snatch a purse." —Carlito, *Carlito's Way*

....

"I want to die a natural death at the age of 102—like the city of Detroit." —Wade Wilson, *Deadpool*

"Eat it till you choke, you sick, twisted f***!" —Paul Sheldon, *Misery*

"I don't like your jerk-off name. I don't like your jerk-off face. I don't like your jerk-off behavior, and I don't like you, jerk-off. Do I make myself clear?"
—Police chief, *The Big Lebowski*

"My God. I haven't been f***ed like that since grade school." —Marla Singer, *Fight Club*

"You shoulda' gone to China. You know, 'cause I hear they give away babies like free iPods. You know they pretty much just put them in those t-shirt guns and shoot them out at sporting events." —Juno MacGuff, *Juno*

"I don't want to talk to you no more, you empty-headed animal food trough wiper. I fart in your general direction! Your mother was a hamster and your father smelt of elderberries!" —French soldier, *Monty Python and the Holy Grail*

"I'm on this new diet. It's very effective. Well, I don't eat anything, and then when I feel like I'm about to faint I eat a cube of cheese. I'm just one stomach flu away from my goal weight." —Emily Charlton, *The Devil Wears Prada*

"You can get a good look at a butcher's ass by sticking your head up there. But, wouldn't you rather take his word for it?" —Tommy, *Tommy Boy*

"I'm going to f***ing make you bend over and I'm gonna reach up your ass into your pocket and get the keys to your house. And then I'm gonna drive there, come in your front f***ing door and kill you in your sleep." —Detective Shannon Mullins, *The Heat*

Sporty
SPOOFS

"I've seen George Foreman
shadow boxing and
the shadow won.**"**

—Muhammad Ali

"Ray Lewis is the type of guy, if he were in a fight with a bear I wouldn't help him, I'd pour honey on him because he likes to fight. That's the type of guy Ray Lewis is."
—Shannon Sharpe, NFL tight end

"He can't kick with his left foot, he can't head, he can't tackle, and he doesn't score many goals. Apart from that, he's all right."
—Soccer player George Best, on David Beckham

"I've had to overcome a lot of diversity." —Drew Gordon, during the NBA draft

"I owe a lot to my parents, especially my mother and father." —Greg Norman, Australian golfer

"I'm traveling to all 51 states to see who can stop 85." —Chad Ocho Cinco, NFL wide receiver

"I feel like I'm the best, but you're not going to get me to say that." —Jerry Rice, NFL wide receiver

"I don't know. I never smoked any Astroturf." —MLB pitcher "Tug" McGraw, on being asked whether he preferred grass or Astroturf

"Any time Detroit scores more than 100 points and holds the other team below 100 points, they almost always win." —Doug Collins, Philadelphia 76ers head coach

"My career was sputtering until I did a 360 and got headed in the right direction." —Tracy McGrath (T-Mac), NBA player

"He's one of the best power forwards of all-time. I take my hands off to him." —Scottie Pippen, NBA star, on Tim Duncan

"Chemistry is a class you take in high school or college, where you figure out two plus two is 10, or something."
—Dennis Rodman, NBA star

"My sister's expecting a baby, and I don't know if I'm going to be an uncle or an aunt."
—Chuck Levitt, NBA player

"I ain't gonna be no escape-goat!" —Karl Malone, two-time NBA MVP

"I'm not an athlete. I'm a professional baseball player."
—John Kruk, first baseman

"He treats us like men. He lets us wear earrings." —Torren Polk, University of Houston wide receiver

"Yankee pitchers have had great success this year against Cabrera when they get him out." —Tim McCorvey, sportscaster and former MLB player

"When you're rich, you don't write checks. Straight cash, homey." —Randy Moss, seven-time Pro Bowl wide receiver

"We must have had 99 per cent of the match. It was the other three per cent that cost us." —Ruud Gullit, Dutch soccer manager and former player

"Yeah, I am lazy. There's no doubt about that."

"If Queen Elizabeth knight hooded me and I would get the title Sir Usain Bolt. That sounds very nice."

—Sprinter Usain Bolt

"I have a tip that can take 5 strokes off anyone's game. It's called an eraser."
—Golfer Arnold Palmer

**"In the end, I am just a guy wearing spandex that turns left really fast."
—Olivier Jean, short-track skater**

"I have been dubbed 'the girl who puts the glamour into hammer.'" —Sophie Hitchon, Olympic hammer thrower

"Pants down in public is not a good idea, it's not good on camera." —Segun Toriola, Nigerian table tennis Olympian, explaining why his team would not repeat a previous medal celebration by collectively pulling down their pants

"Because there are no fours."
—Antoine Walker, 2006 NBA champion, when asked why he shoots so many three-pointers

"I believe I am more intelligent than the average person. There are few people with such talent, so there are few able to judge what I am doing." —Mario Balotelli, Italian soccer player, on his antics involving throwing darts at youth league players and sneaking into a women's prison

"My wiener has never been so exhausted." —Kurt Busch, NASCAR driver, after winning the Oscar Mayer Wienermobile race

"Well, either side could win it, or it could be a draw." —Ron Atkinson, English soccer manager and former player

'It ain't the heat. It's the humility." —Yogi Berra, Yankee legend

"If someone is too perfect they won't look good. Imperfection is important."

"Sometimes you get submerged by emotion. I think it's very important to express it—which doesn't necessarily mean hitting someone."

"We won the European Championship last September and now the world title. That is some year for French beach soccer! Now comes the hard part. We have to keep improving and that's difficult because it's tough to do better than winning a world title."

"I prefer to play and lose rather than win, because I know in advance I'm going to win."

—Eric Cantona, French soccer player

"Something will pop up in my head. It could be like the weirdest thing. Like all of a sudden like I have like a jumping banana in my head. And I stop and pause. I'm like that damn banana is in my head. Like, I don't know what's going on."

"You can tell a great athlete by like not how many times he wins unlike when he loses, because that's what's gonna make a swimmer."

—Ryan Lochte, Olympic swimmer

% &!*

"The goal was scored a little bit by the hand of God, another bit by the head of Maradona." —Soccer star Diego Maradona, after scoring with his hand during the World Cup

"I'm rich. What am I supposed to do, hide it?" —Lou Whitaker, MLB All-Star, after taking a stretch limo to a players' union meeting during the 1994 baseball strike

"Raise the urinals." —Darrel Chaney, announcer and former shortstop, on how the Atlanta Braves' coaches could keep the players on their toes

"Therapy can be a good thing; it can be therapeutic." —Alex Rodriguez, 14-time All-Star third baseman

"Surprise me." —Yogi Berra, Hall of Fame catcher, when asked by his wife where he wanted to be buried

"Ninety percent of the game is half mental." —Jim Wohlford, MLB outfielder

"Having a record company and putting out my own CD. There's clothes and shoes. There's also an upcoming book deal that I'm trying to do. I'm trying to be positive. I'm a big fan of the Nobel Peace Prize." —Metta World Peace, 2004 NBA Defensive Player of the Year

....

"He's the Man of the Hour, at this particular moment." —Don King, boxing promoter

....

"Every time that I have ever tried to help a woman out, I have been incarcerated." —Jose Canseco, 1988 MLB MVP

"I want to rush for 1,000 or 1,500 yards, whichever comes first." —George Rogers, 1980 Heisman Trophy–winning running back

"It's not like we came down from Mount Sinai with the tabloids." —Ron Meyer, former Indianapolis Colts head coach, on whether his staff could lead the Colts to the promised land

"I want all the kids to copulate me." —Andre Dawson, Chicago Cubs Hall of Famer on the need to be a role model

"I can't really remember the names of all the clubs we went to." —Shaquille O'Neal, NBA champion, in reference to being asked if he'd been to the Parthenon while in Greece

"You can sum up this sport in two words...You never know." —Lou Duva, boxing trainer

"Fade into Bolivian, I guess." —Mike Tyson, on what he'd do after retiring from boxing

"Well, Rickey's not one of them, so that's 49 percent right there." —Rickey Henderson in response to the suggestion that 50 percent of MLB players use steroids

"Sometimes you see beautiful people with no brains. Sometimes you have ugly people who are intelligent, like scientists."

"Please don't call me arrogant, but I'm European champion and I think I'm a special one."

"Unhappy is a nice word."

"For me, your real age is not the age on your ID. That's just a date when you were born."

—José Mourinho, Portuguese soccer manager and former player

"I can go right, I can go left, I'm amphibious." —Charles Shackleford, NBA power forward

"The sun has been there for 500, 600 years." —Mike Cameron, three-time Gold Glove outfielder

---

"We didn't underestimate them. They were a lot better than we thought." —Bobby Robson, English soccer player

---

"I don't want to shoot my mouth in my foot, but those are games we can win." —Sherman Douglas, NBA player

"God created the sun, the stars, the heavens and the earth, and then made Adam and Eve. The Bible never says anything about dinosaurs. You can't say there were dinosaurs when you never saw them. Someone actually saw Adam and Eve. No one ever saw a Tyrannosaurus rex." —Carl Everett, MLB World Series champion

"They shouldn't throw at me. I'm the father of five or six kids." —Tito Fuentes, MLB player

"The doctors X-rayed my head and found nothing." —Dizzy Dean, baseball legend

"I do not like this word 'bomb.' It is not a bomb. It is a device that is exploding." —Jacques LeBlanc, boxer

"I'm the oldest I've ever been, right now." —Tim Sylvia, mixed martial arts fighter

"The drivers have one foot on the brake, one on the clutch and one on the throttle." —Bob Varsha, motorsports announcer

"In his interviews, [David] Beckham manages to sit on the fence very well and keeps both ears on the ground." —Brian Kerr, director of St. Patrick's Athletic football club

"I love Fidel Castro, I respect Fidel Castro, you know why? A lot of people have wanted to kill Fidel Castro for the last 60 years, but that motherf****er is still here." —Ozzie Guillen, MLB shortstop, in 2012 (Castro died in 2016)

"I've been dunked on by Potapenko and now Tabak. The good part is that they don't make posters of those guys." —Walt Williams, NBA player

"I enjoyed the Luge." —Michael Jordan, on the Louvre in Paris

"Ball handling and dribbling are my strongest weaknesses." —David Thompson, NBA player

"Ladies, here's a hint. If you're up against a girl with big boobs, bring her to the net and make her hit backhand volleys. That's the hardest shot for the well-endowed." —Tennis player Billie Jean King

"I've won at every level, except college and pro." —Shaquille O'Neal, four-time NBA champion

"I spent 90% of my money on women and drink. The rest I wasted." —George Best, soccer player for Manchester United

"Like they say, it ain't over 'til the fat guy swings." —Darren Daulton, Phillies catcher, on stocky first baseman John Kruk

"We have a great bunch of outside shooters. Unfortunately, all our games are played indoors." —Weldon Drew, college basketball coach

"I definitely want Brooklyn to be christened, but I don't know into what religion yet." —David Beckham, on the birth of his first son

"We didn't lose the game; we just ran out of time." —Vince Lombardi, football coach

....

"Yeah, I regret we weren't on a higher floor." —Charles Barkley, NBA analyst and former player, on whether he had any regrets about throwing a bar patron through a first-floor window

....

"He is one of the most known athletes in the world and a lot of impact in any kind of sport that he did. Even playing hockey, everyone knows him. From being the type of person he was off the ice and on the ice. It's unfortunate that he passed away a year ago, but you know he changed a lot while he was with us. He's a tremendous guy." —Jonathan Bernier, NHL goaltender, honoring Nobel Peace Prize winner Nelson Mandela

"I can't help but laugh at how perfect I am."

"Absolutely not. I have ordered a plane. It is much faster." (on rumors he had bought a Porsche)

"One thing is for sure. A World Cup without me is nothing to watch."

"We're looking for an apartment. If we don't find anything, then I'll probably just buy the hotel." (on being humble)

"When you buy me, you are buying a Ferrari."

"Come over to my house baby, and bring your sister. I'll show you who's gay."

"I didn't injure you on purpose and you know that. If you accuse me again I'll break both your legs, and that time it WILL BE on purpose."

—Zlatan Ibrahimovic, Swedish soccer star

"I knew when my career was over. In 1965 my baseball card came out with no picture." —Bob Ueker, former MLB player, coach, and actor

"The last time the Cubs won the World Series was 1908. The last time they were in one was 1945. Hey, any team can have a bad century. —Tom Treblehorn, MLB manager

"Baseball is 90% mental, the other half is physical." —Yogi Berra, legendary MLB catcher

"Aw, how could he lose the ball in the sun? He's from Mexico." —Harry Caray, former Cubs announcer, on Jorge Orta losing track of a fly ball

"I'm tired of hearing about money, money, money, money. I just want to play the game, drink Pepsi, wear Reebok." —Shaquille O'Neal, four-time NBA champion

"I disagree with his lifestyle. I do disagree with the fact that Billy is a homosexual. That doesn't mean I can't still invest in him and get to know him. I don't think the fact that someone is a homosexual should completely shut the door on investing in them in a relational aspect. Getting to know him. That, I would say, you can still accept them but I do disagree with the lifestyle, 100 percent."
—Daniel Murphy, Mets infielder, on Billy Bean, the first MLB player to come out as gay, in the 1990s

"I quit school in the 6th grade. Not because I had it, but because I couldn't spell it." —Rocky Graziano, boxing champion

"I managed a team that was so bad we considered a 2-0 count a rally."
—Rich Donnelly, MLB coach

"Let that be a lesson to you all. Nobody beats Vitas Gerulaitis 17 times in a row." —Vitas Gerulaitis, on beating tennis star Jimmy Connors after losing 16 straight matches to him

"I've been in the twilight of my career longer than most people have had their career." —Martina Navratilova, tennis player

"I was point shaving." —Kobe Bryant, NBA player, on missing three free throws at the end of a win in 2011

"I don't want to sound like I'm pontificating or anything but I think I'm really good at that. I'm the best. Besides Versace, Armani, I'm right up there." —Serena Williams, tennis player, on her skills as a fashion designer

"I can play in the center, on the right, and occasionally on the left side." —David Beckham, soccer player, when asked if he was a "volatile" player

....

"I made a 1,600 minus 800 minus 200 on the SAT, so I'm very intelligent when I speak." —Shaquille O'Neal, four-time NBA champion

....

"I'll be sad to go, and I wouldn't be sad to go. It wouldn't upset me to leave St. Louis, but it would upset me to leave St. Louis. It's hard to explain. You'll find out one of these days, but maybe you never will." —Brett Hull, NFL Hall of Famer

"Now, I'm not doctor or anything, but I'm pretty sure death is always serious." —Alan Minter, middleweight champion addresses the dangers of boxing

"I have a family to feed…If [team owner Glen Taylor] wants to see my family fed, he better cough up some money. Otherwise, you're going to see these kids in one of those Sally Struthers commercials soon." —Latrell Sprewell, NBA player, trying to work out a contract extension with the Timberwolves; Sprewell turned down a $21-million offer and expressed how it insulted him

....

"We're not really going to worry about what the hell [the fans] think about us. They really don't matter to us. They can boo us every day, but they're still going to ask for our autographs if they see us on the street. That's why they're fans, and we're NBA players." —Bonzi Wells, NBA player

....

"I think that if rape is inevitable, relax and enjoy it." —Bob Knight, legendary NCAA basketball coach, when asked how he dealt with stress

"I would retire first. It's the most hectic, nerve-racking city. Imagine having to take the 7 train to the ballpark, looking like you're [riding through] Beirut next to some kid with purple hair next to some queer with AIDS right next to some dude who just got out of jail for the fourth time right next to some 20-year-old mom with four kids. It's depressing…The biggest thing I don't like about New York are the foreigners. I'm not a very big fan of foreigners. You can walk an entire block in Times Square and not hear anybody speaking English. Asians and Koreans and Vietnamese and Indians and Russians and Spanish people and everything up there. How the hell did they get in this country?"
—John Rocker, Atlanta Braves pitcher, when asked if he would ever consider playing in New York

"It's not going to be peaches and gravy all the time." —Brad Miller, NBA player, describing the team's struggles

"It's almost like we have ESPN or something." —Magic Johnson, on how he and teammate James Worthy always work so well together on the court

"I may be dumb, but I'm not stupid." —Terry Bradshaw, NFL analyst and former player

"People think we make $3 million and $4 million a year. They don't realize that most of us only make $500,000." —Pete Incaviglia, Texas Rangers outfielder

"That's all they said was wrong with me?" —Mike Tyson, heavyweight champ, responding to questions about his problems with depression, low self-esteem, and anger management

"Why should we have to go to class if we came here to play FOOTBALL, we ain't come to play SCHOOL, classes are POINTLESS." —Cardale Jones, Ohio State backup quarterback, on Twitter

"We're leaving a big fat rail of coke and a shot of Jack for Santa this year... cookies and milk will just slow him down. #SimpleTruth" —Patriots linebacker Brandon Spikes, tweeting during the holidays

"Oh, $120,000." —Hensley Meulens, MLB outfielder, after being asked what he had gotten out of his rookie season in the league

"I don't have the first clue who he is talking about, because all I worry about is Jerome." —Jerome James, Seattle SuperSonics center, explaining his views on why his coach called him selfish

"Gaylord Perry and Willie McCovey should know each other like a book. They've been ex-teammates for years now." —Jerry Coleman, San Diego Padres broadcaster

"Sam is an idiot—I-D-O-U-T—idiot." —Shaquille O'Neal, on *Chicago Tribune* writer Sam Smith, who wrote an article suggesting the Miami Heat rid themselves of "The Big Aristotle"

"It may not impress you, but Holtz means 'hard wood.'" —Lou Holtz, former college football coach and television analyst

"I'm very appreciative of being indicted." —Bill Peterson, former Florida State football coach, on being inducted into the Florida Hall of Fame

"It has not been proven, but I think it will be proven that the air is thinner now, there have been climactic changes over the last 50 years in the world, and I think that's one of the reasons balls are carrying much better now than I remember." —Tim McCarver, sportscaster, on increased home run rates in the MLB

"Better make it six. I can't eat eight." —Dan Osinski, MLB pitcher, after a waitress asked him if he wanted his pizza cut into six slices or eight

"I've only scratched the iceberg." —Andre Agassi, tennis star, assessing his talent ceiling in 1990

"Great trade! Who did we get?" —Lenny Dykstra, Philadelphia Phillies outfielder, after hearing an unproductive member of the team had been traded away

"He's a guy who gets up at six o'clock in the morning regardless of what time it is." —Lou Duva, boxing trainer, on training heavyweight Andrew Golota

"I don't think anyone on this team knows what 'schism' is, let alone could use it in a sentence. I thought it was an STD when I first heard it and was like 'whoa, we preach abstinence in these parts.'" —Jared Allen, Vikings defensive end, about the possibility of a hostile schism growing in the locker room between teammates

"Anyone with knowledge of the slave trade and the NFL could say that these two parallel each other." —Rashard Mendenhall, Pittsburgh Steelers player, on Twitter

"We're not attempting to circumcise the rules." —Bill Cowher, former NFL head coach

"Ancient gravity was much weaker...Gravity had to be weaker to make dinosaurs nimble."
—Jose Canseco, MLB outfielder

**"I love the tension. I love when everything's going wrong...In the NBA, they don't promote guys like me. They like guys who like Cheerios, good guys. But I find a way to promote myself."
—Metta World Peace, NBA Defensive Player of the Year**

"To win, I'd run over Joe's mom, too." — Matt Millen, NFL linebacker, after Redskins lineman Joe Jacoby stated he'd "run over my own mother to win the Super Bowl"

"Joe Frazier is so ugly he should donate his face to the US Bureau of Wildlife." —Muhammad Ali

"Because she is too ugly to kiss goodbye." — Bum Phillips, NFL coach, on why he brings his wife on road trips

"Yeah, I'm cocky and I am arrogant. But that doesn't mean I'm not a nice person."
—Jeremy Roenick, NHL center

**"What problems do you have, apart from being blind, unemployed and a moron?"
—John McEnroe, to a Wimbledon spectator**

....

"When you say I committed adultery, are you stating before the marriage of 1996 or prior to?" —Deion Sanders, Dallas Cowboys cornerback

....

"Saltwater taffy." —Caldwell Jones, NBA player, on his favorite seafood

"It's a humbling thing being humble."
—Maurice Clarett, Ohio's Mr. Football 2001, after finding out his draft stock had dropped

Miscellaneous Thinkers
& CREATIVE
TYPES

"Let me be clear about this:
I don't have a drug problem,
I have a police problem."

—Keith Richards

"The supposed astronomical proofs of the theory [of relativity], as cited and claimed by Einstein, do not exist. He is a confusionist. The Einstein theory is a fallacy. The theory that ether does not exist, and that gravity is not a force but a property of space can only be described as a crazy vagary, a disgrace to our age." —Charles Lane Poor, American astronomer

"A theory should not attempt to explain all the facts, because some of the facts are wrong." —Francis Crick, one of the discoverers of the structure of DNA

"I have eaten many strange things, but have never eaten the heart of a king before." —English theologian William Buckland, who loved eating unusual meat. According to the writer Augustus Hare, he was once shown "the heart of a French King preserved at Nuneham in a silver casket. And, before anyone could hinder him, he had gobbled it up, and the precious relic was lost forever."

"We need a program of psychosurgery for political control of our society. The purpose is physical control of the mind. Everyone who deviates from the given norm can be surgically mutilated...The individual may think that the most important reality is his own existence, but this is only his personal point of view. This lacks historical perspective. Man does not have the right to develop his own mind. This kind of liberal orientation has great appeal. We must electronically control the brain. Someday armies and generals will be controlled by electric stimulation of the brain."
—Professor José Delgado, Yale University

"What a strange thing man is; and what a stranger thing woman." —Lord Byron

"Properly read, the Bible is the most potent force for atheism ever conceived." —Isaac Asimov

"Medical scientists are nice people, but you should not let them treat you." —August Karl Gustav Bier, German surgeon, the first to perform spinal anesthesia and intravenous regional anesthesia

"I hight don Quixote, I live on peyote, marijuana, morphine and cocaine. I never know sadness, but only a madness that burns at the heart and the brain. I see each charwoman, ecstatic, inhuman, angelic, demonic, divine. Each wagon a dragon, each beer mug a flagon that brims with ambrosial wine." —Jack Parsons, rocket scientist

"The feeling is constantly growing on me that I had been the first to hear the greeting of one planet to another."

"The scientists of today think deeply instead of clearly. One must be sane to think clearly, but one can think deeply and be quite insane."

"The trend of opinion among eugenists is that we must make marriage more difficult. Certainly no one who is not a desirable parent should be permitted to produce progeny."

—Nikola Tesla,
scientist and inventor

"My music is best understood by children and animals." —Igor Stravinsky

"What you are, you are by accident of birth; what I am, I am by myself. There are and will be a thousand princes; there is only one Beethoven." —Ludwig van Beethoven

....

"I may not be a first rate composer, but I am a first-class second-rate composer." —Richard Strauss

....

"Time is a great teacher, but unfortunately it kills all its pupils." —Hector Berlioz

"What the world needs is more geniuses with humility. There are so few of us left." —Oscar Levant

"If you wait for inspiration to write, you're not a writer, you're a waiter." —Dan Poynter

"One can't judge Wagner's opera Lohengrin after a first hearing, and I certainly don't intend hearing it a second time."
—Gioachino Rossini, on Richard Wagner

**"Listening to the fifth symphony of Ralph Vaughan Williams is like staring at a cow for 45 minutes."
—Aaron Copland, on Vaughan Williams**

"She's only pretty in that she has two small black eyes and a good figure." —Wolfgang Amadeus Mozart, on his future wife, Constanze

"Write to me and don't be so lazy. Otherwise I'll have to give you a thrashing. What fun! I'll break your head." —Mozart, to his sister

"He was a six and a half foot scowl."
—Igor Stravinsky, on Sergei Rachmaninov

"All music is folk music. I ain't never heard a horse sing a song." —Louis Armstrong

"All the good music has already been written by people with wigs and stuff."

"Jazz is not dead, it just smells funny."

"Rock journalism is people who can't write interviewing people who can't talk in order to provide articles for people who can't read."

—Frank Zappa

"I don't know anything about music. In my line you don't have to." —Elvis Presley

"If I didn't do this well, I just wouldn't have anything to do...I can't cook, and I'd be a terrible housewife." —Freddie Mercury, Queen

"I'm sick to death of people saying we've made 11 albums that sound exactly the same. In fact, we've made 12 albums that sound exactly the same." —Angus Young, AC/DC

"There are two golden rules for an orchestra: start together and finish together. The public doesn't give a damn what goes on in between." —Thomas Beecham

"There are two kinds of artists left: those who endorse Pepsi and those who simply won't." —Annie Lennox

"I've been imitated so well I've heard people copy my mistakes." —Jimi Hendrix

"After I saw Jimmy [Hendrix] play, I just went home and wondered what the f*** I was going to do with my life."
—Jeff Beck

"Actually I don't remember being born, it must have happened during one of my blackouts." —Jim Morrison

"I don't deserve a Songwriters Hall of Fame Award. But fifteen years ago, I had a brain operation and I didn't deserve that, either. So I'll keep it!" —Quincy Jones

"I smash guitars because I like them." —Pete Townshend

"I never had much interest in the piano until I realized that every time I played, a girl would appear on the piano bench to my left and another to my right." —Duke Ellington

"Dogs smoke in France." —Ozzy Osbourne

"When I was a little boy, I told my dad, 'When I grow up, I want to be a musician.' My dad said: 'You can't do both, Son.'" —Chet Atkins

"If you're listening to a rock star to get your information on who to vote for, you're a bigger moron than they are." —Alice Cooper

"To get your playing more forceful, hit the drums harder." —Keith Moon

"Sometimes we pee on each other before we go on stage." —Trent Reznor, Nine Inch Nails

"I think John would have liked Free As A Bird. In fact, I hope somebody does this to all my crap demos when I'm dead, making them into hit songs." —George Harrison

"In the end we're all Jerry Springer Show guests, really, we just haven't been on the show." —Marilyn Manson

"If I knew I had to play this song the rest of my life I probably woulda wrote something else…." —Joe Walsh, on "Rocky Mountain Way"

"When an instrument fails on stage it mocks you and must be destroyed!" —Trent Reznor

"Too many pieces of music finish too long after the end." —Igor Stravinsky

"I never practice my guitar…from time to time I just open the case and throw in a piece of raw meat." —Wes Montgomery

"Writer's block is a fancy term made up by whiners so they can have an excuse to drink alcohol." —Steve Martin

"People think that I must be a very strange person. This is not correct. I have the heart of a small boy. It is in a glass jar on my desk." —Stephen King

"Suppose you were an idiot. And suppose you were a member of Congress. But then I repeat myself."

"If voting made any difference they wouldn't let us do it."

"The Bible. It is full of interest. It has noble poetry in it; and some clever fables; and some blood-drenched history; and some good morals; and a wealth of obscenity; and upwards of a thousand lies."

"Of all the things I've lost, I miss my mind the most."

"Religion was invented when the first con-man met the first fool."

"But who prays for Satan? Who, in eighteen centuries, has had the common humanity to pray for the one sinner that needed it most?"

—Mark Twain

Caustic, Crazy & Cutting
CRIMIMALS

"Sometimes I feel like God…
when I order someone killed—
they die the same day.**"**

—Pablo Escobar

"I punched my mother out once."
—Charles Manson

"I like children, they are tasty." —Albert Fish, aka the Gray Man, the Werewolf of Wysteria, the Brooklyn Vampire, the Moon Maniac, the Boogey Man. He boasted that he "had children in every state."

"What's one less person on the face of the earth, anyway?"

"We serial killers are your sons, we are your husbands, we are everywhere. And there will be more of your children dead tomorrow."

—Ted Bundy, serial killer

"I would cook it, and look at the pictures and masturbate."

"I've got to start eating at home more."

—Jeffrey Dahmer, aka the Milwaukee Cannibal, serial killer and sex offender

"I robbed them, and I killed them as cold as ice, and I would do it again, and I know I would kill another person because I've hated humans for a long time." —Aileen Wuornos, serial killer

"The only one that can do what I do is me. Lot of people had to die for me to be me. You wanna be me?" —Frank Costello, crime boss

"She isn't missing. She's at the farm right now." —Ed Gein, murderer and grave robber

"Guns are neat little things, aren't they? They can kill extraordinary people with very little effort." —John W. Hinckley Jr., who tried to assassinate President Ronald Reagan

"I rob banks for a living, what do you do?"

"All my life I wanted to be a bank robber. Carry a gun and wear a mask. Now that it's happened I guess I'm just about the best bank robber they ever had. And I sure am happy."

"These few dollars you lose here today are going to buy you stories to tell your children and great-grandchildren. This could be one of the big moments in your life; don't make it your last!"

—John Dillinger, gangster

"I will have you removed if you don't stop. I have a little system of my own." —Charles Manson

"When I killed people I had a desire [to kill more]. This inspired me to kill more. I don't care whether they deserve to live or not. It is none of my concern." —Yang Xinhai, serial killer, China

"I felt pleasure, even though when I had killed, the guilt came over me." —Luis Garavito, aka the Beast, Colombian rapist and serial killer

"It was only good if I could see her eyes." —Pedro Alonso Lopez, aka the Monster of the Andes

"You have to be like a lion and a fox. The fox is smart enough to recognize traps, and the lion is strong enough to scare away the wolves. Be like a lion and a fox, and no one will beat you." —Carlo "Don Carlo" Gambino, Italian-born American gangster

> **"There can only be one king."**
>
> "I prefer to be in the grave in Colombia than in a jail cell in the United States."
>
> —Pablo Escobar,
> Colombian drug lord

"Weapons are an extension of my body. Like my arms. I learned that at training camp in the Bekaa Plain. I also learned that to kill, you have to act fast and aim straight at the nose."
—Ilich Ramírez Sánchez, aka Carlos the Jackal, Venezuelan-born international terrorist

"I supply more heroin, methamphetamine, cocaine, and marijuana than anybody else in the world. I have a fleet of submarines, airplanes, trucks, and boats." —Joaquin "El Chapo" Guzman

"You can get much farther with a kind word and a gun than you can with a kind word alone."

"I got nothing against the honest cop on the beat, the kind you can't buy. You just have to have them transferred someplace where they can't do you any harm."

"I'm a kind person, I'm kind to everyone, but if you are unkind to me, then kindness is not what you'll remember me for."

"Some call it bootlegging. Some call it racketeering. I call it a business."

"We been on the road for 18 hours...I need a bath, some chow...and then you and me sit down, and we talk about who dies, eh?"

"Now I know why tigers eat their young."

—Al Capone, gangster

"There is nothing wrong with Mr. Kraft's mind other than that he likes killing for sexual satisfaction." —Prosecution for Randy Kraft, serial killer

"What I did was not for sexual pleasure. Rather it brought me some peace of mind." —Andrei Chikatilo, aka the Maniac, Russian serial killer

"We love death. The US loves life. That is the difference between us two."

"We are continuing this policy in bleeding America to the point of bankruptcy. Allah willing, and nothing is too great for Allah."

—Osama bin Laden

"My mother was cancer. She slowly destroyed everything around her. She produced two killers; me and my brother Joe." —Richard "Iceman" Kuklinski

"Gun control? It's the best thing you can do for crooks and gangsters. I want you to have nothing. I'm a bad guy; I'm always gonna have a gun. Safety locks? You will pull the trigger with a lock on, and I'll pull the trigger. We'll see who wins."

"Never open your mouth, unless you're in the dentist chair."

"I loved the Godfather. I thought that was the best interpretation of our life that I've ever seen. Godfather I and Godfather II—the other one stunk."

—Salvatore "Sammy the Bull" Gravano, former underboss of the Gambino crime family

"We took care of Kennedy." —Salvatore "Mooney Sam" Giancana, better known as Sam Giancana, Sicilian American mobster

"Assassin?...That sounds so exotic...I was just a murderer." —Richard "Iceman" Kuklinski, American contract killer, known for his method of freezing a victim to mask the time of death

"May your wife and children get raped, right in the ass." —Aileen Wuornos, serial killer, to the jurors who convicted her

"I was raised to be a rugged, strong-minded hustling type of woman so you can throw me in this concrete jungle with nothing and I'll still come out fed with a lion on my back." —Griselda Blanco, aka the Black Widow

Blunt Business
TYCOONS

"A squirrel dying in front of your house may be more relevant to your interests right now than people dying in Africa."

—Mark Zuckerberg

"I don't think anybody should write his autobiography until after he's dead."
—Samuel Goldwyn

"Pretty much, Apple and Dell are the only ones in this industry making money. They make it by being Wal-Mart. We make it by innovation." —Steve Jobs

"The only meat I eat is from animals I've killed myself." —Mark Zuckerberg

"We've got to pause and ask ourselves: How much clean air do we need?" —Lee Iacocca

"Be fearful when others are greedy and greedy when others are fearful." —Warren Buffet

"Bury your mistakes." —Rupert Murdoch

"Part of the beauty of me is that I am very rich." (speaking on *Good Morning America*)

"No, I'm not into anal." (speaking on *The Howard Stern Show*)

"Sorry losers and haters, but my I.Q. is one of the highest—and you all know it! Please don't feel so stupid or insecure, it's not your fault" (on Twitter)

"Listen, you motherf***ers, we're going to tax you 25 percent!" (referring to China in 2011)

"Ariana Huffington is unattractive both inside and out. I fully understand why her former husband left her for a man—he made a good decision."

"I don't want to use the word 'screwed' but I screwed him." (on renting land to Muammar Qaddafi, on *Fox and Friends*, 2011)

—Donald Trump, American tycoon and president

"The debt is like a crazy aunt we keep down in the basement. All the neighbors know she's there but nobody wants to talk about her."
—Ross Perot

"We don't break the law."
—Kenneth Lay, CEO of Enron

"We don't pay taxes. The little people pay taxes."

"I'm a very firm believer that a liar is a cheat and a thief and a crook. I don't like liars. I never lie. I always told my own child, 'If you murder somebody, tell me. I'll help you hide the body. But don't you lie to me.'"

"Money enhances a man, yes, as beauty enhances a woman."

—Leona Helmsley

"Of course I know how to roll a joint."

"I think that people want to know how to do practical and everyday things like how to get the pomegranate seeds out of a pomegranate."

"I have a microphone on one ankle and an ankle bracelet on the other, so I'm well balanced today."

"The last place I would ever want to go is prison."

"Am I the same girl? Yes, I am... Although I have changed."

"As with all my new pets, I gently bit each kitten on the face. This is how I let my animals know that I am now their mother."

"I think you can fairly say I spawned or laid an egg that has turned into a lifestyle industry."

—Martha Stewart

"She just needs to be quiet. She's a movie star. If she were confident in her acting, she wouldn't be trying to be Martha Stewart."
—Martha Stewart, on Gwyneth Paltrow

"I've got a virtually limitless supply of bullsh*t."

"If people get all the sex they can handle, they're so happy and content they just sit around and smile. I mean, you never feel aggressive just after you've gotten laid, right? Lots of sex for everybody, that's a solution to the world's problems."

"My son is now an 'entrepreneur.' That's what you're called when you don't have a job."

—Ted Turner

"The way to make money is to buy when blood is running in the streets." —John D. Rockefeller

"The indictment, in a lot of ways, that was the turning point." —Jeffrey Skilling, chairman of Enron

"Most of us don't invent ideas. We take the best ideas from someone else."

"In the beginning, I was so chintzy I really didn't pay my employees well."

"Give ordinary folk the chance to buy the same things as rich people."

—Sam Walton, Walmart founder

"Play off everyone against each other so that you have more avenues of action open to you."

"Every man has his price, or a guy like me couldn't exist."

"I'm not a paranoid deranged millionaire. Goddamit, I'm a billionaire."

"We don't have a monopoly. Anyone who wants to dig a well without a Hughes Bit can always use a pick and shovel."

"God took away my parents, but I've saddled myself with another burden."

"His ears made him look like a taxicab with both doors open."

—Howard Hughes

"Buy old masters. They fetch a better price than old mistresses."
—Max Aitken, Canadian-British business tycoon, politician, newspaper publisher, and writer

INDEX